# Antiquities of the [...] of Kerry

JASON BOLTON

**Word**well

First published in 2008
Wordwell Ltd
PO Box 69, Bray, Co. Wicklow
Copyright © The author

All rights reserved. No part of this book may be reprinted or reproduced or utilised in any electronic, mechanical or other means, now known or hereafter invented, including photocopying and recording, or otherwise without either the prior written consent of the publishers or a licence permitting restricted copying in Ireland issued by the Irish Copyright Licensing Agency Ltd, The Writers' Centre, 19 Parnell Square, Dublin 1.

ISBN 978-1-905569-27-4

British Library Cataloguing-in-Publication Data.

A catalogue record for this book is available from the British Library.

This publication has received support from the Heritage Council under the 2008 Publications Grant Scheme.

Typeset in Ireland by Wordwell Ltd

Copy-editor: Emer Condit

Printed by Castuera, Pamplona

# ANTIQUITIES OF THE RING OF KERRY

# Contents

| | |
|---|---|
| Acknowledgements | vii |
| Introduction | 1 |
|     The Kerry landscape | 1 |
|     The prehistoric period | 2 |
|     The early medieval period | 8 |
|     The later medieval period | 10 |
| **Site gazetteer** | 12 |
| KILLARNEY NATIONAL PARK | 12 |
|     Innisfallen Abbey | 13 |
|     Ross Castle | 15 |
|     Muckross Abbey | 17 |
| Lissyvigeen stone circle | 18 |
| Kenmare stone circle and boulder burial | 18 |
| Cromwell's Bridge, Kenmare | 19 |
| Dunkerron Castle and fortified house | 20 |
| Derrynabla rock art | 21 |
| Parknasilla/Sneem shipwreck | 23 |
| Staigue stone fort | 23 |
| Children's burial-grounds | 25 |
| Castlecove Castle | 26 |
| Coomnahorna and Garrough stone alignments | 28 |
| Ballycarnahan Castle | 29 |
| Derrynane caher | 30 |
| Derrynane ogham stone | 31 |
| Ahamore Abbey, Abbey Island | 32 |
| Derrynane cannons | 33 |
| Loher stone fort | 33 |
| Eightercua stone row | 34 |
| Dromkeare stone row | 35 |
| Ballinskelligs Castle and abbey | 36 |
| The Skelligs | 38 |
| VALENTIA ISLAND | 39 |
|     Glanleam standing stone | 40 |
|     Cool East wedge tomb | 40 |
|     Illaunloughan monastic site | 41 |

|  |  |
|---|---|
| Cromwell's Fort | 41 |
| Valentia slate quarries | 42 |
| Cahergal stone fort | 42 |
| Leacanabuile stone fort | 44 |
| Ballycarbery hall-house | 45 |
| Kealduff Upper rock art | 46 |
| Cloonmore megalith | 47 |
| Dunloe ogham stones | 48 |
| Aghadoe round tower and Romanesque church | 48 |
| Parkonavear Anglo-Norman castle | 50 |
|  |  |
| References | 52 |

# ACKNOWLEDGEMENTS

No matter which road you take in Kerry, there always seems to be a castle or church or ancient tomb somewhere nearby. Over the years I've been fortunate to explore the shores, the mountains and the sea surrounding the Ring of Kerry for both work and recreation, and would like to both acknowledge and thank the following people and organisations:

The Heritage Council, who commissioned Sara Pavía and me to undertake a second 'Stone Monuments Study' to examine the deterioration of stone monuments on the Atlantic seaboard of Cork, Kerry and Donegal in 2002. My most grateful thanks to Charles Mount, and later Ian Doyle, Archaeology Officers with the Heritage Council.

Una Cosgrave, Heritage Officer with Kerry County Council, who asked us to conserve a pair of carved Valentia slate benches now preserved in Tralee Public Library.

Paul McMahon and John Cahill of the Office of Public Works and Mr Gerry Stanley of the Geological Survey of Ireland, who provided the opportunity to re-examine Staigue fort in 2007.

Michael Connolly, County Archaeologist, for the opportunity to consider the conservation of Ballycarty passage tomb in 2006.

Dr Pat Dargan, Dr Sara Pavía, Gerry Walker and the Dublin Institute of Technology, who made it possible to explore the world of stone monuments and the conservation of coastal archaeology as part of doctoral research.

Professor John Ashurst, who very kindly asked me to contribute to his *Conservation of ruins*, in which Ballinskelligs Castle plays a prominent role.

Teresa Zille, who worked wonders with my collection of photographs of the antiquities of Kerry, editing, tweaking and photoshopping mercilessly through the thousands of photos.

The staff of Tralee Library for providing access to their wealth of local history information.

Dublin University Sub-Aqua Club for their introduction to coastal and underwater Kerry, beginning with a storm-blown diving trip in 1994 which turned into a rainy exploration of the slate town of Knightstown and the local history museum.

The Irish Maritime Archaeology Society: Andrew Thoma, who arranged underwater archaeological projects on the Derrynane cannons (which he discovered in 1991), the Skelligs and the wreck of the *Elizabeth Anne* at Parknasilla; Deirdre O'Hara, who arranged a photographic survey of the cannon wreck as part of a TG4 series on historic shipwrecks; and the late Robin Leigh for his enthusiasm and unique perspective on maritime archaeology.

The final thanks are to my Mam, Harriett Ledwidge, for a rainswept childhood tour of the Killarney lakes, and choppy boat rides in 1998 to Fungie and Innisfallen; to my Dad, Robert Bolton; and especially to my sons, Daragh and Mattia, who still enjoy lost ruins in the countryside once there's a picnic and games.

# INTRODUCTION

**The Kerry landscape**

The Ring of Kerry, also known as Iveragh, is the largest peninsula and the most mountainous area in Ireland. The landscape is wild, dominated by mountain ranges cut by steep-sided valleys, cliffs, pockets, glens and narrow passes, a varied coast stretching from sandy bays at Ballinskelligs and Derrynane to high sea-cliffs and long sandy spits, and bogs found to the north and west of the mountains. This diverse landscape has been shaped by glacial action on the underlying rocks. Most of the rocks on the Iveragh peninsula are part of the Old Red Sandstone, masses of sand and gravel cemented into rock about 370 million years ago. Igneous rocks are also found near Valentia, surrounded by purple siltstones (quarried as slate), which is found throughout Valentia Island, and on the mainland from Puffin Sound to Cahersiveen. After the retreat of the glaciers, vegetation began to become firmly established in Kerry from about 10,000 years ago. The coastline has changed shape, with sea levels rising from 10–16m below what we see today, resulting in widespread inundation and coastal erosion. Remnants of submerged forests and peatland from these former shorelines can be seen during low tides in the sands of Ballinskelligs Bay. Grassy meadows were quickly colonised by juniper, willow and birch, and then taller trees gradually became established. Seven thousand years ago the uplands were filled with birch and pine, while the coastal lowlands were covered by a dense, tall, deciduous forest of oak, elder, hazel and elm. This was the landscape encountered by the earliest

**Above left:** Eightercua stone row.

**Above right:** Leacanabuile stone fort.

**Left:** Entrance to Staigue fort (Wilkinson 1845).

hunter-gatherers to explore the Iveragh peninsula—a wild landscape continuing to take shape, an unexplored land of primeval forests, of boar, bear, wildcat, fox and wolf, a new land to challenge any explorer.

**The prehistoric period**

The further back we go in time, the harder it is to find traces and to build a picture of what life was like for the first colonisers of Kerry. The earliest evidence for human colonisation/habitation in Kerry, and indeed in Ireland, comes from the Mesolithic period (c. 7500–4500 BC) after the retreat of the glaciers at the end of the last Ice Age. As the climate improved, a greater variety of vegetation and wild animals encouraged early hunter-gatherers to explore the landscape, and traces of their lives have been found along the coast, on islands and in caves. The early hunters and foragers probably existed as small bands, not interfering with the primeval forest cover and living on a varied diet that included wild pig, fish, seal, shellfish and a variety of birds. Flint tools were used, but it is probable that most of the fishing, hunting and foraging equipment was made from wood, feathers, gut and other organic materials. Coastal settlement between 4600 and 3800 BC at Ferriter's Cove on the nearby Dingle peninsula and a 6,500-year-old stone platform buried within the peat on Valentia Island provide the earliest evidence for humans in Kerry. The beach areas of Ballinskelligs Bay show peat layers and submerged forests that may also contain Mesolithic remains, constantly washed by the passing tides. Blanket bog is one of the characteristics of the landscape of the west of Ireland, formed over the millennia as a result of forest clearance and fluctuations in climatic conditions. The bogs seen along the Ring of Kerry have formed over a long period; bog on Valentia Island has been dated to over 6560 ± 120 years BP (before present), though some of the bogs began to form more recently.

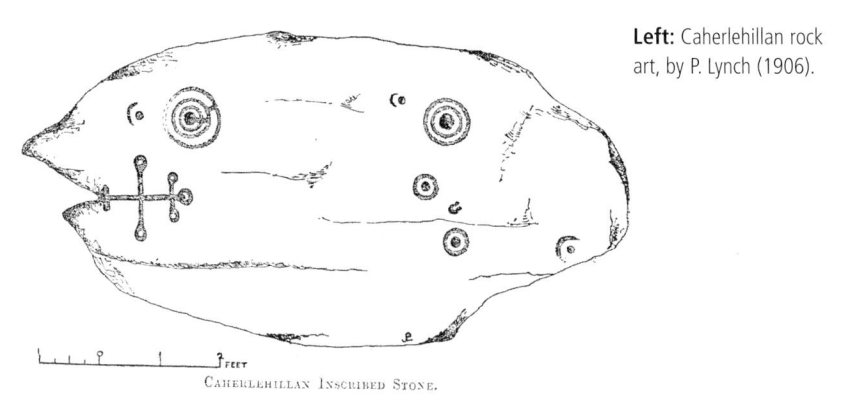

**Left:** Caherlehillan rock art, by P. Lynch (1906).

CAHERLEHILLAN INSCRIBED STONE.

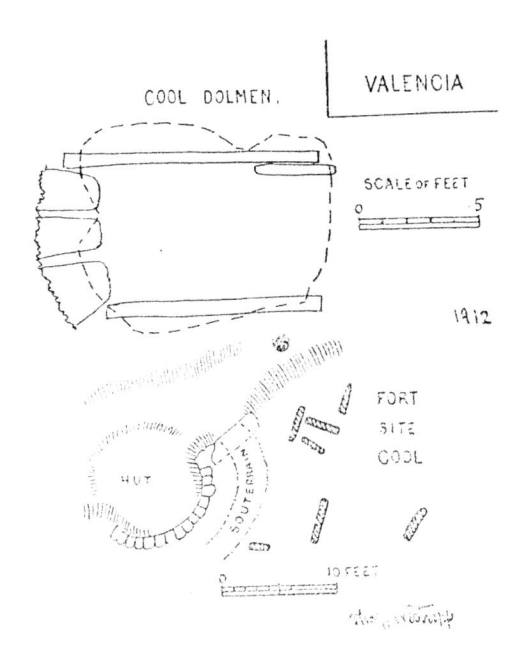

**Left:** 'Dolmen and Fort at Cool', by Thomas Westropp (1912).

The earliest settlers in Ireland gradually turned to farming, and raising animals and growing cereals became central to their way of life. This period, the Neolithic (*c.* 4600–2500 BC), saw the first human-induced changes to the landscape, with the clearance of sections of forest for grasslands, the construction of settlements, houses and field systems, and a focus on commemorating the dead through the construction of megalithic tombs. Neolithic field walls buried under blanket bog are known from Valentia Island and these are usually seen as evidence for a pastoral farming way of life; the study of pollen records suggests that increasing woodland clearance and the creation of grasslands around Killarney in the third millennium BC is best associated with the expansion of farming. Stray finds of Neolithic artefacts, including stone axeheads and arrowheads, have also been found, showing that hunting and warfare probably continued throughout Irish prehistory. Some of the megalithic wedge tombs (from the Greek *megas* 'great' and *lithos* 'stone') found on the peninsula may date from the late Neolithic, though these types of burial monuments were also used in the Bronze Age. These tombs are the physical expression of a cult of the dead that spread among early agricultural communities, and have links to similar monuments on the Atlantic seaboard of Europe, extending from Scandinavia to Portugal.

The introduction of metal into Ireland was an important change, and was accompanied by new materials, culture and burial traditions in a period known as the Bronze Age (*c.* 2400–600 BC). It is in the Bronze Age that we begin to see the development of ritual monuments, tombs, houses and settlement on the Ring of Kerry. Most of the Bronze Age monuments on the Ring of Kerry commemorate the dead or

**Left:** Rock art at Kealduff Upper.

**Above:** The double lintel above the doorway to Staigue fort.

are ritual monuments. Wedge tombs, boulder burials and a number of unclassified tombs are found on the peninsula. Stone circles, stone rows, stone pairs and single standing stones are also common. The stone rows are usually aligned to events in the lunar or solar calendar; for example, the row at Eightercua points to the setting sun at the winter solstice. Stone alignments and circles (such as Lissyvigeen or the 'Seven Sisters', near Killarney) are believed to date from between 1700 and 800 BC, and may have had some related ceremonial and ritual purpose. Bronze Age settlement in the area is known from a few excavated sites such as Coarha More on Valentia Island, where archaeological excavation uncovered the remains of a stone hut dating from *c.* 800 BC, with a central timber post to support the roof, cut into the developing bog. The hut had a drainage system to bring

**Left:** Map of promontory forts from St Finan's Bay to Doulus Head, by Thomas Westropp (1912).

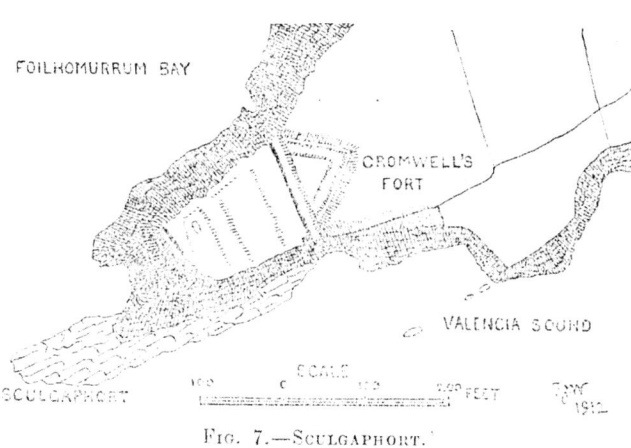

**Left:** 'Cromwell's Fort' at Sculgaphort overlooking Valentia Sound, by Thomas Westropp (1912).

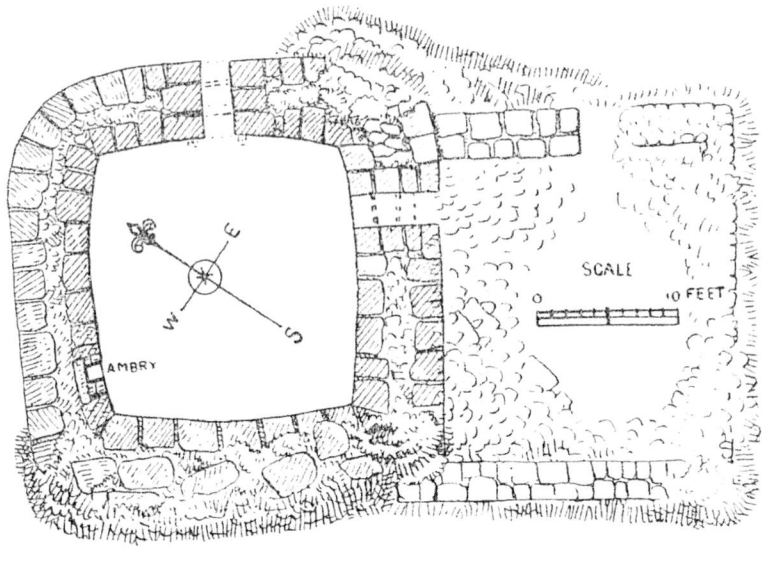

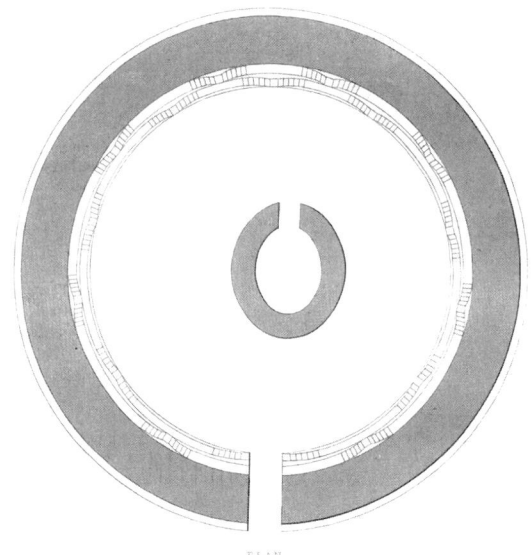

**Above:** Plan of *clochán* on Bray Head, Valentia Island, by Thomas Westropp (1912).

**Left:** Plan and cross-section of Cahergal fort (Wilkinson 1845).

water away from the hut, and traces of worked wood, flint and pottery were also found. Systems of fields and rectangular huts buried beneath peat that began to form towards the end of the Bronze Age suggest that cattle were becoming increasingly important. Settlement on the peninsula was probably also encouraged by the mineral wealth of the area.

The term 'Bronze Age' refers to the emergence of the considerable technological achievement of converting rock to metal for the production of weaponry, tools, ornaments, jewellery and utensils. With its significant gold and copper resources, Ireland's importance in early prehistoric Europe is indicated by the wide range of copper, bronze and gold objects found in the country. Ross Island in Lough Leane contains the earliest known copper-mines in western Europe, dating from 2400–1900 BC. The first copper objects probably arrived from mainland Europe, possibly as gifts or through exchange. The copper ores of the south-west of Ireland were soon located, however, and were worked to extract the valuable metal. The Ring of Kerry is a particularly rich source of ore, found on the shores of Lough Leane, on Coad Mountain, at Staigue, Derrynane, Lambs Head, Little Skellig and on Valentia Island, and a number of primitive mine sites are known on the peninsula. The early miners used simple stone tools, fire and ingenuity to extract the ore, crush and sort it, and then smelt the mineralised rock fragments as part of a process of learning to refine, alloy and cast molten copper. The National Museum of Ireland has recorded many bronze artefacts from the Ring of Kerry, including copper and bronze axeheads, halberds (or blades), spearheads, a bronze trumpet-horn from Derrynane, a bronze sword from Valentia Island, pins and daggers.

The availability of new tools, weapons and goods in the Bronze Age was accompanied by the development of new types of building and monument. Hillforts began to emerge, as well as a host of enigmatic monuments such as stone and timber circles, stone alignments and standing stones, enclosures, burial mounds and boulder monuments. This building activity was accompanied by changes to the landscape, with a steady rate of woodland clearance for agriculture. Bronze Age settlement appears as circular enclosures containing small groups of circular buildings, though unenclosed settlements are also known. *Fulachta fiadh*, low mounds of burnt stones and charcoal, were very common in the Bronze Age, and are most often considered to have been cooking-places.

Stone huts, both circular and rectangular, are found throughout the Ring of Kerry. Many different types of stone hut are known, dating from prehistory to the modern day, and huts of timber, sod and wattle are also known. The best-known type is the beehive hut or *clochán*, which has a corbelled stone roof, though other huts with corbelled walls and flat lintels are also known. Some of the best-preserved examples, with simple rectangular doorways, are found on Skellig Michael. Without excavation it is not usually possible to date a hut simply by looking at it, but the occurrence of large numbers of corbelled huts at ecclesiastical sites and ringforts suggests that they may have been a common form of dwelling in the early medieval period. The relatively few excavated huts, such as the *clochán* at Coarhabeg on Valentia Island, dating from between the sixth and eighth centuries, have yielded early medieval dates.

These huts, however, may have been used both earlier and later. The hut sites found on the hills and uplands may be related to 'booleying' or transhumance, a system whereby families moved their cattle to summer pastures in the mountains, returning home in time for the autumn harvest.

The last prehistoric period is the Iron Age (*c.* 600 BC–AD 400), marked by the use of iron for weapons, jewellery, tools and utensils and by a change in Irish culture. The Iron Age has historically been an obscure period in Ireland's past, though archaeological excavation is uncovering more about this 'dark age'. Alongside the continued use of hillforts, Iron Age sites show a number of new introductions, including linear earthworks, rotary querns for milling, large decorated stones and a focus on warfare and weapons. Iron Age burials have proved difficult to locate; it is possible that some bodies were not buried and that other rites, such as the scattering of ashes, were used. Several types of burial monument are known, however, such as ring-barrows, ring-ditches, mounds and enclosures.

**The early medieval period**

Ireland was never invaded by the Romans and continued as a rural, tribal-based society throughout the Iron Age and into the early medieval period. The earliest Christian missionaries arrived in a world of warfare, slavery, kidnapping and ransom, cattle raids and the emergence of new assertive dynasties dominating a society without towns, without money, and virtually illiterate. The country was divided into numerous kingdoms and local groups called *tuath*. The most common settlement was the earthen ringfort or the stone caher, which were enclosed farmsteads. The larger stone forts were more elaborate versions of the simple caher, and probably represent the dwellings of the local élite. The construction of so many of these structures was accompanied by an explosion in agricultural activity based on cereal-growing and animal husbandry. Many of these structures were also used for more specialised purposes, such as the production of textiles, glass and metals.

Christianity had arrived in Ireland by the fifth century, brought by missionaries such as Palladius, sent in 431 to 'the Irish believing in Christ', the famous St Patrick, who left a documentary account of his mission in his *Confession* and *Epistle to Coroticus*, and many others such as Sechnaill and Ciaran. The early church set up parishes and a diocesan system, but by the sixth century monasticism had become widespread. Both systems existed side by side for a time, but gradually the role of the bishops lessened and the church was controlled by the abbots of the more important monastic centres. Many of these monastic settlements began as self-sufficient eremetic communities, generally surrounded by an outer enclosure, the *vallum*, with

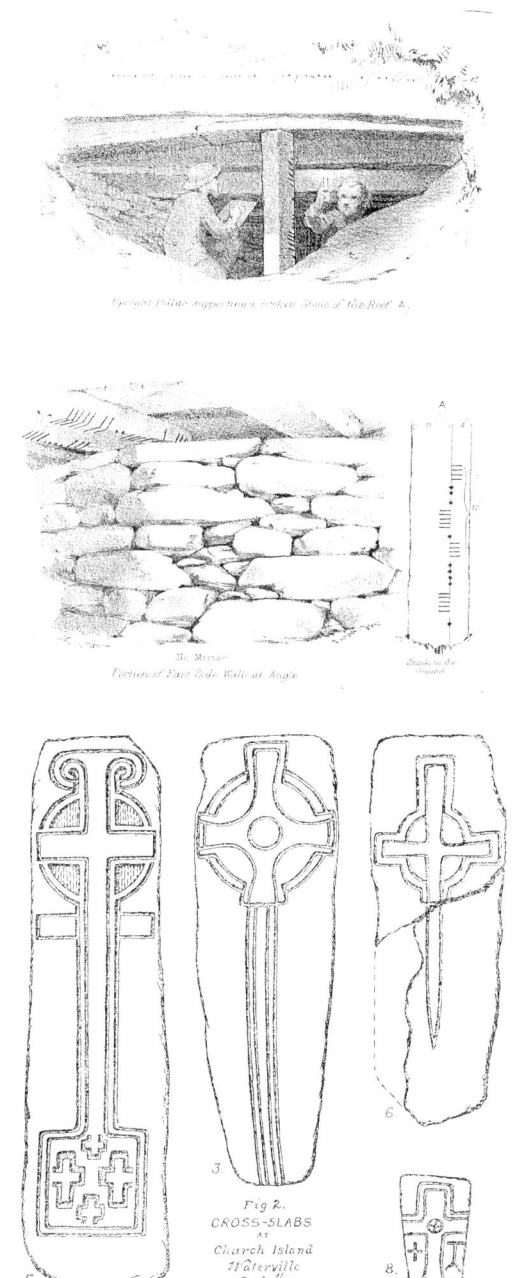

**Top:** The Dunloe ogham stones, as found reused as roof lintels in a souterrain by J. Rhys (1903).
**Above:** 'Cross-slabs at Church Island, Waterville' (Crawford 1926).

an inner enclosure surrounding the church and graveyard. A wide range of sites existed, however, from large religious and political centres to small isolated hermitages. Very few of these sites, with the exception of hermitages such as the Skelligs, are in remote places. The majority are usually located on good agricultural land in areas of dense secular settlement. From the seventh century onwards, these sites produced much of the ecclesiastical art and architecture familiar to us today, such as illuminated manuscripts, carved sculpture, stone buildings and intricate metalwork such as the Ardagh Chalice and various reliquaries and shrines.

The earliest churches were of timber, and no trace of these survives above ground level. The earliest stone churches probably date from the ninth century; these are single-chamber buildings with a single window in the east elevation and a lintelled doorway in the west elevation or at the west end of the south elevation. Irish churches are normally aligned east–west. The earliest churches may also feature antae (extensions of the side walls beyond the gables in imitation of elbow-cruck timber construction) and cyclopean masonry. Ecclesiastical sites along the

Ring of Kerry often feature stone huts and oratories and a wide range of smaller stone features, including ogham stones, crosses, fonts, cross-slabs, pillars, cross-inscribed stones, grave-slabs and *leachta* or gable-shrines. Some of the most notable early ecclesiastical settlements of the Ring of Kerry are isolated eremetical monasteries, often located on islands. These include Church Island near Waterville, Illaunloughan beside Valentia Island, and the Skelligs.

**The later medieval period**

The Ring of Kerry is far from the centres of Viking activity in Ireland, though the monastery on the Skelligs was raided twice in the ninth century. The next major change occurred in the twelfth century with the establishment of the diocesan and parochial system in the Irish church at the synods of Rathbreasil and Kells. The Iveragh peninsula was divided into eleven parishes as part of the deanery of Aghadoe in the diocese of Ardfert. This had a major impact on the monastic settlements on the peninsula, many of which gradually fell out of use. This period also saw the introduction of Romanesque art at Church Island near Waterville, at Aghadoe and at Innisfallen. The twelfth century also saw the introduction of Continental orders of

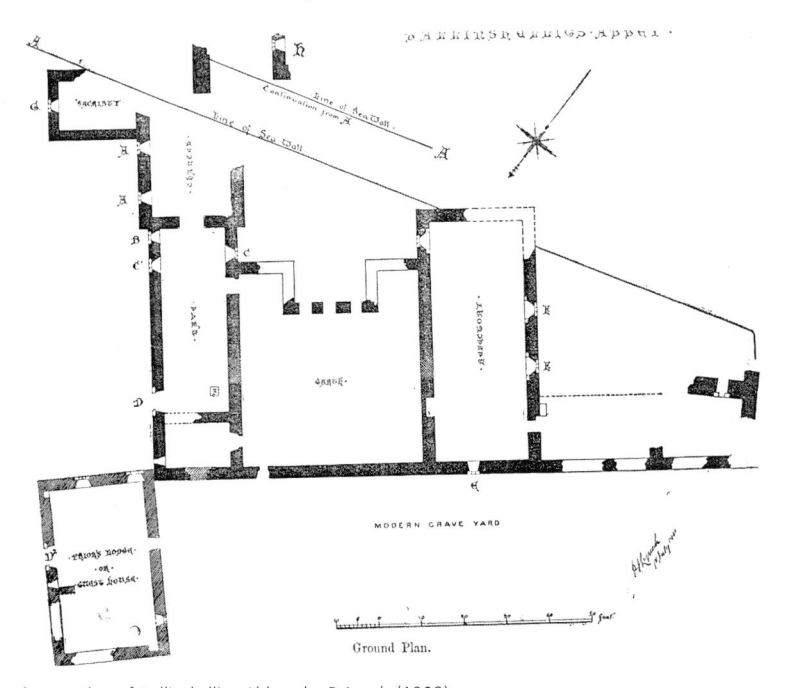

**Above:** Plan of Ballinskelligs Abbey, by P. Lynch (1902).

monks into Ireland, including the Cistercians, Franciscans, Augustinians, Benedictines, Carmelites and others. The new friaries and abbeys of these orders were arrangements of specially adapted structures, including a large church with refectory, dormitories, chapter house and other offices arranged around a quadrangular cloister, normally located to the south of the church. These complexes were often later repaired and added to, especially during the fifteenth century. Like the earlier monastic sites, these new establishments, such as the Augustinian abbey at Ballinskelligs, were expected to be self-sufficient, and an ecclesiastical complex might include a guest-house, brewery, bakery, granary, school, mill and fish-traps.

Most of later medieval Ireland was dominated by the impact of the Anglo-Normans, who established fiefs, towns, a monetary system and a new political system. During the early medieval period the Iveragh peninsula was dominated by two main dynasties, the Corca Dhuibhne and the Eóganacht Locha Léin. The Anglo-Norman conquest of Ireland caused many dynasties and septs to reorganise and many to be displaced to search for new lands. The O'Sullivans and their overlords the McCarthys migrated in the twelfth century from their ancestral lands to south Munster, depriving natives of the peninsula such as the O'Sheas and the O'Falveys of their land. After the victory of the McCarthy and Desmond septs at the Battle of Callan in 1261, the Ring of Kerry was to remain under Gaelic lordship during much of the later medieval period. Parkonavear is the only Anglo-Norman castle marked in the site gazetteer below. The other tower-houses and fortified houses strung along the coast were held by the O'Sullivans, the O'Donoghues and the McCarthys. The dissolution of the monasteries in 1536–40, followed by Cromwell's campaign a century later, resulted in widespread change to the Ring of Kerry, with the destruction and abandonment of ecclesiastical sites and the replacement of the Gaelic rulers by new lords such as Sir William Petty.

**Left:** Muckross Abbey, Killarney National Park.

# SITE GAZETTEER

*The Ring of Kerry is one of Ireland's best-known tourist trails, starting from Killarney and circling the Iveragh peninsula through Kenmare, Sneem, Waterville and Cahersiveen. The Ring is very busy in summer, and all tour buses run anti-clockwise, as many sections of the route are too narrow to allow two buses to pass. The archaeological sites suggested below lie along the Ring of Kerry, ordered as if travelling in a clockwise direction to avoid the heavy traffic flow.*

## THE KILLARNEY NATIONAL PARK AREA

The native woodlands, blanket bog, heath, lakes, rivers and streams of Lough Leane have attracted settlers for over 4,000 years, and the area now forms the core of the Killarney National Park. The Park lies immediately south of Killarney, covering over 25,000 acres including Lough Leane, Muckross Lake and the Upper Lake, and comprises the former Muckross Estate and the Kenmare Estate. Amidst and surrounding the park, and under the backdrop of the Magillicuddy Reeks, are a range of prehistoric and medieval sites and buildings dating back at least 4,000 years. Copper-mines at Ross Island are dated to the beginning of the Bronze Age (*c.* 2400–1800 BC), and are widely recognised as the oldest mines in north-west Europe. The limestone rocks at the edge of the lakes hold a streak of minerals, including copper, lead, zinc, silver and cobalt, which were mined in at least four locations at different times from the Bronze Age to the medieval period to the modern age, before being abandoned around 1830.

Mesolithic remains were recently discovered on the shores of Ross Island, in the form of a Bann flake, a broad-bladed stone tool (*c.* 7000–4000 BC), found in shoreline spoil from eighteenth- and nineteenth-century mining operations. A wide range of other prehistoric and medieval sites can be found in and around the park, including a *fulacht fiadh* (an ancient cooking-place) at Ballydowney and an Early Christian period souterrain (underground chamber) at Dundag beside Muckross Lake. At Cloghmochuda, close to Knockreer House, is a stone with two hollows in its surface. Originally this was probably a bullaun stone and used for grinding corn, but it has become associated with the legend of Cuddy and is visited as a place of healing. The battlefield of Tooreencormick, on the slopes of Mangerton, was the site of the last unsuccessful attempt by the Anglo-Normans to wrest control of the Ring of Kerry and west Cork from the McCarthys, Gaelic overlords of Desmond. Individual archaeological finds are also known from the area, with the topographer Samuel Lewis writing in 1837:

'A very curious relic of antiquity, in form resembling a kettle-drum, was found some years since in a bog near Muckross; it is of bronze, about two feet in diameter, and on being struck emits a deep-toned, hollow sound, resembling that of the Indian gong; it is deposited in the library of Charlemont House, Dublin. A smaller one, which was found near it, was broken in attempting to raise it.'

The remains of the McCarthy Mór castle of Castlelough can be seen on the shoreline in the grounds of the Lake Hotel. The lowlands to the east of Lough Leane hold the Bronze Age stone circle of Lissyvigeen, standing stones and traces of ringforts. The lake area holds some of the most impressive and most accessible antiquities of the Ring.

**Innisfallen Abbey**

Monastic sites are the main source of evidence for Early Christian activity around the Ring of Kerry. One of the most important of these sites was the monastery founded in the seventh century on the island of Innisfallen (*Inis Faithleann*) in Lough Leane and dedicated to St Fionán. The island is large enough to have allowed the monks to remain relatively self-sufficient, providing timber and fertile soil for crops, space for livestock and fish from the lake. The island was the birthplace of the famous Annals of Innisfallen, written between the eleventh and thirteenth centuries, described by the nineteenth-century antiquarian Samuel Lewis as

**Left:** Innisfallen Abbey (courtesy of the National Library of Ireland).

**Above:** Innisfallen Island (courtesy of the National Library of Ireland).

> 'an ancient manuscript, containing a general history of the world, from the creation to the year 430 of the Christian era, but thenceforward confined to the history of Ireland'.

Lewis described the island as

> 'the most beautiful and interesting of all in the Lower Lake; it is extremely fertile and richly clothed with wood to the water's edge; among various trees of stately growth is a holly, of which the stem is fourteen feet in girth'.

The island features a rich collection of monastic buildings, including two twelfth-century churches—one with an ornate Romanesque doorway built with yellow and red sandstone, and the other with a simple round-headed door with inclined jambs. Another Romanesque building, possibly the library scriptorium, has a famous Romanesque carved head, thought to be a representation of St Fionan, and a Romanesque chancel arch. The riches of the church made it a target for periodic raids, with the Annals of Innisfallen describing an attack in 1180: 'Innisfallen was plundered by Mal Duin, son of Donal O'Donoghue, and much gold, and silver was taken out of the church'. The monastery of Innisfallen developed further after 1197, when it became the Augustinian Priory of St Mary; some structures were extended and a range of new buildings, such as the cloister, kitchen, refectory and dormitory, were added. Here in the priory the Annals of Innisfallen, one of the most important sources for Irish history, were compiled until the early fourteenth century.

## Ross Castle

Ross Castle is an imposing late fifteenth-century tower-house overlooking Lough Leane and the isthmus leading to Ross Island. It consists of a large, rectangular tower-house or keep, surrounded by a fortified enclosure known as a bawn or a ward, with a curtain wall defended by circular flanking towers, two of which are still standing. Tower-houses like this were constructed mainly in the fifteenth and sixteenth centuries as fortified residences for local Irish and Old English families and display many of the defensive features of earlier castles.

**Above:** Ross Castle, by Mary Herbert (courtesy of the National Library of Ireland).

The defences of Ross Castle included an entrance protected by a yett (a metal grille pulled up by chains to protect the main oak door), with a confined entrance hall with a 'murder hole' above and a guardroom to the right. Bartizans (or overhanging turrets), crenellated battlements and a machicolation allowed defence from the wall-tops; the walls were provided with arrow and gun loops, and a base batter protected them from undermining. The different floors of the keep are connected by a stone spiral staircase, leading to the vaulted bedchamber, the garderobe (the toilet, accessed through a narrow corridor off the stairs) and the great hall. The great hall was the centre of activity in Ross Castle, with a large open fireplace, a kitchen, a minstrels' gallery and lit by two large six-light windows.

The castle was originally the defensive residence of one of the O'Donoghue Ross chieftains. Between 1568 and 1583 the O'Donoghue Ross rose in rebellion with the

**Above:** Ross Castle after its recent conservation works.

**Left:** Ross Castle, by Gabriel Beranger (courtesy of the National Library of Ireland).

earl of Desmond against Elizabeth I, resulting in the loss of both his life and his lands when the rebellion was put down, and ownership eventually passed to Sir Valentine Browne, the surveyor-general of Ireland. In 1641 rebellion broke out again, this time against Charles I, but it was not until after the execution of the king in 1649, marking the end of the English Civil War, that the Parliamentary army under Cromwell arrived in Ireland to regain control. In the 1640s and 1650s Ross Castle was held by both

Catholic Confederate and Cromwellian forces. Samuel Lewis noted: 'Here are the picturesque ruins of Ross castle, founded by the O'Donoghues; it was defended by Lord Muskerry against the parliamentarians in 1652, and surrendered to Ludlow', referring to the siege of Ross Castle. General Ludlow brought 4,000 soldiers and 2,000 cavalry to Kerry, and Ross Castle was one of the last strongholds to fall during the Cromwellian wars. Lord Muskerry was forced to surrender when Ludlow brought cannon through the River Laune and across Lough Leane, reputedly fulfilling a local prophecy that the castle would not fall 'until a ship would swim upon the lake'. In the late seventeenth century a fortified house ('The New Court') was built beside the tower-house ('the old castle') by Sir Valentine Browne (later Lord Kenmare), the grandson of the surveyor-general. After the Williamite wars the castle became a permanent garrison barracks, with new buildings built in the mid-eighteenth century to accommodate the governor and two companies of infantry. Ross Castle acted as a garrison until 1825, after which it passed back into the hands of Lord Kenmare. The tower has been undergoing conservation works for some years and is open to visitors. This tower-house can be compared with the fragments of the McCarthy Mór castle, originally associated with the demesne lands of Muckross, surviving on a promontory on the shore of Lough Leane in the grounds of the Lake Hotel.

**Muckross Abbey**

The abbey, once known as the Franciscan friary of Irrelagh (*oir bhealach* or 'eastern pass'), was founded *c*. 1448 by a local Gaelic lord, Donal McCarthy Mór. It is a fine, well-preserved example of later medieval church life, and the burial place of local chieftains and the poets Geoffrey O'Donoghue, Aodhagan O'Rathaille and Eoghan Ruadh O'Suilleabhain. In 1837 Samuel Lewis wrote that:

> 'This abbey, formerly called Irrelagh, was founded by Donald, son of Thady McCarthy, in 1440, and has since continued to be the favourite place of sepulture of that family; it was rebuilt in 1626, but was soon afterwards suffered to fall into decay; it consisted of a nave, choir, transept and cloisters, which last are still nearly entire. The entrance is through a pointed doorway, of which the arch is deeply moulded; and a narrow pointed archway leads into the choir, in which are the tombs of the McCarthy Mores and the O'Donoghues of the Glens: there is also a large mural monument to the wife of Christopher Galway, Esq., beautifully executed in Italian marble.'

The abbey also contains grave-slabs, an armorial stone and a holy tree. The friary is built to a planned layout of a church with a belfry tower located between the nave and the choir. The now-lost high altar of the choir was located beneath the four-light Gothic limestone window, but the piscina, the tombs and the pointed archway leading to the sacristy allow an understanding of this most sacred part of the church, which was reserved for the use of the friars. The tower separating the nave from the choir is found in friaries throughout the country, though the one at Muckross is unusual owing to its width, as most towers taper to form a high, slender feature above the roof. The cloister, located to the north of the church, is formed by four well-lit vaulted passages (the ambulatory) around a square courtyard with a deliberately planted yew tree in the centre. The cloister is surrounded by buildings: the church to the south, an east range showing traces of wickerwork on the plastered vault of the ceiling, a north range with storerooms on the ground floor and the refectory above, and the west range, which features a spacious private apartment with many windows and a large fireplace. The friary at Muckross fell into decline during the late fifteenth century; there was probably little to suppress during the dissolution of the monasteries ordered by King Henry VIII in 1540, and the friars appear to have remained at Muckross. In the late sixteenth century the friary began its passage to private ownership, leased initially to the earl of Clancarty in 1587 and to Captain Robert Collam in 1595, and eventually passing to the earl of Kenmare. The friars returned in the early seventeenth century and began to restore the buildings, but were periodically evicted until the friary was burnt by Cromwellian forces in 1652.

**Lissyvigeen stone circle**

This well-known small stone circle is formed of seven low upright stones, sometimes called *dallan* stones, in the centre of a circular earthwork, with a stone pair, marked as *gallauns* on early maps, to the south-west. The outlying stones and the stone circle form an alignment with Torc and Mangerton mountains to the south-west. A drawing by G. M. Atkinson from 1884 shows the stone circle in an open rural landscape, with Flesk Castle, Killarney town and the lower lake in the background. The stone circle has been closed to the public for the past few years, but permission can be obtained from the landowner.

**Kenmare stone circle and boulder burial**

Stone circles are circular or subcircular arrangements of free-standing upright stones, usually with an astronomical alignment. Irish stone circles are concentrated in two

**Above:** Kenmare stone circle and boulder burial.

main groups—one in Ulster and the other in counties Cork and Kerry. The stone circle at Kenmare overlooks the River Finnehy in a well-kept modern garden, and is probably the largest in south-west Ireland. It is formed by thirteen upright and two flat (or prostrate) stones, and is known locally as 'the Shrubberies'. The circle features an axial stone set opposite the pair of portal stones, and a line drawn between them would point to the setting sun in the south-west. The circle is unusual as it also contains a central Bronze Age boulder burial, one of over 80 examples known. Boulder burials are concentrated in the south-west of Ireland, mainly in west Cork. These tombs were not covered with a mound of earth or stones like the earlier megalithic monuments. The cover-stone at the Shrubberies rests on three low stones; it is approximately 2.8m long, 1.8m wide and 0.8m thick, and probably weighs about seven tons.

**Cromwell's Bridge, Kenmare**

The town of Kenmare contains a possibly medieval bridge crossing the River Finnehy on the old border between the baronies of Dunkerron South and Glanarought. Cromwell's Bridge survives as a semicircular arch barrel above the tidal stretch of the Finnehy, but no spandrel walls, wing walls, parapet or road surface remain. The majority of extant bridges in Ireland date from the late eighteenth and nineteenth

**Left:** 'Cromwell's Bridge', Kenmare.

centuries. Few earlier bridges have survived, and the most common cause of destruction is flooding. Traces of early bridges can be found underwater, such as the eighth-century wooden bridge at Clonmacnoise, Co. Offaly, but most of the earliest Irish bridges, such as King John's Bridge at Esker, Co. Dublin, are in a similar state to Cromwell's Bridge. This is a 'pack-horse' bridge, standing almost 6m high, built of wedge-shaped stones with an arch span of 5m. The name 'Cromwell' may be derived from the Irish word *croiméal*, meaning 'moustache', or from *croim* ('stooped') *maol* ('bald'), meaning a bridge without a parapet.

**Dunkerron Castle and fortified house**

This castle is best known as the principal seat of the O'Sullivan Mores, who ruled over half of the Iveragh peninsula during the later medieval period. The history of the castle is unclear, although it was reputedly rebuilt in the mid-fifteenth century and added to in 1596, before eventually being burnt by Lord Muskerry in 1646 to prevent its capture by advancing Cromwellian forces. Dunkerron Castle is built on a rocky limestone knoll in the grounds of Dunkerron House, overlooking Kenmare Bay to the south. It survives as the remains of a tall tower-house, surrounded by a holiday-home complex. The tower appears cracked open, with only the north wall standing to full height, allowing us to see the interior. The walls are 2.6m thick at ground level but gradually become thinner towards the top—a feature common to the tower-houses seen circling the Ring of Kerry. The base of the tower also tapers out, forming a sloped surface called a batter, which is a common defensive feature of medieval castles. Like Ross Castle, Dunkerron has the remains of a defensive bawn wall and a fortified turret at the south-west angle, which was accessible from the tower-house at first-floor level.

The tower-house has kept many of its details, including stepped battlements on the top of the wall and stair passages contained within the thickness of the walls. The cold, grey limestone walls would originally have been plastered inside and out with an off-white lime plaster, which helped to insulate the building and its inhabitants from the extremes of the weather. The original ground-floor entrance was located at the south and was approached from within the defensive wall or bawn. The internal timber floors of the castle would have been carried on stone corbels, some of which can still be seen protruding from the surface of the wall.

The remains of the fortified house, Dunkerron Court, are located approximately 20m to the east of the tower-house. Fortified houses are a group of buildings built over a period of approximately 60 years during the late sixteenth and early seventeenth centuries. The period began with the construction of Rathfarnham Castle, Co. Dublin, *c.* 1590 by Adam Loftus. The fortified houses were roomier, better-lit and more comfortable than tower-houses, whose role they began to take over. These houses retained defensive features such as flanking towers, machicolations, bartizans and gun loops, but their primary function was residential, with the emphasis on more comfortable and luxurious living. Defensive features of Irish fortified houses could include gun loops and enclosing bawn walls, possibly with a gatehouse and mural towers. Fortified houses vary in shape, but were usually three storeys high and set out to a regular rectangular plan. Only one wall of Dunkerron Court survives, standing three storeys high with a gabled attic with square stone chimney-pots. A 2.4m-wide fireplace from one of the main first-floor rooms can be seen on the interior wall. Like the tower-house, the internal timber floors were carried on stone corbels, which are still visible amid the vegetation clinging to the stone walls.

**Derrynabla rock art**

The carved decoration on the rocky slopes of Derrynabla constitutes some of the best-known prehistoric art in Ireland. The practice of carving designs on stone is common to many periods and cultures across the globe, and is usually termed rock art, rock carving or petroglyphs. The limited range of rock art motifs found in Ireland are shared with the countries of Atlantic Europe, including Portugal, Spain, France, Britain and Scandinavia. Rock art in Ireland is mainly concentrated in the Dingle and Iveragh peninsulas of County Kerry, although groups are also known from Donegal, Louth and elsewhere. Most examples in Kerry occur in elevated positions overlooking river valleys or the sea. These carvings are normally found on rock outcrops and small boulders. Irish rock art has parallels with the range of motifs found

**Left:** Derrynabla rock art overlooking the Kealduff River valley.

on passage graves, and the petroglyphs also occur on wedge tombs, cist graves and standing stones. This type of art is believed to date from the late Neolithic or early Bronze Age, but there are difficulties in dating it.

Irish rock art motifs include cup marks, cup and ring marks, circles and concentric circles as well as some angular motifs. The commonest design is the cup mark (a circular depression *c*. 2–5cm in diameter), usually enclosed by one or more concentric circles. Radial lines often run across or through gaps in the circles. The carving was carried out with a hard stone point hammered to form pick marks, but is also occasionally incised. The meaning and purpose of rock art motifs are unknown, but suggestions have included some ritual function, maps of settlements or field systems, astronomical markings, and early metallurgists' marks.

The rock art at Derrynabla is located at the head of the Kealduff River valley, surrounded by the Mullaghanattin, Knockaunanattin and Knocklomena mountains, and overlooking Lough Brin to the east. The art can be difficult to find, on a slope of blanket bog with rock outcrops and boulders, but is well worth the effort. The

Derrynabla group of 26 rock art carvings is the largest individual concentration of these prehistoric carvings identified in Ireland to date. It includes 23 cup marks and eighteen cup and ring motifs on a massive, regularly shaped, elongated sandstone boulder half-buried in the hillside and measuring approximately 3.5m long and 2.5m wide. The decorated stone lies on a mountain slope approximately 2km east of Pocket Mountain. At the west end of this boulder is a smaller stone known as the 'Derrynabla Shield'. About 200m east of these two stones is a low rock decorated with cup marks and concentric grooves, and a standing stone can be seen further to the east.

**Parknasilla/Sneem shipwreck**

No one knows how many ships were wrecked on the shores of Ireland over the last few thousand years, but known wrecks number over 15,000, ranging from prehistoric log boats, medieval ships and the Spanish Armada wrecks to the merchantmen, warships and submarines of the twentieth century. The location of island hermitages around the Ring of Kerry and the construction of tower-houses around the coast of the Iveragh peninsula indicate the enduring importance of seaborne travel and trade. A relatively recent shipwreck is that of a Glasgow schooner, the *Elizabeth Anne*, which left Kenmare in ballast for Caernarfon on 27 January 1903. A force 10 storm blew up, and when the ship anchored in Kenmare Bay the anchors dragged and the schooner was wrecked close to the Parknasilla Hotel. Today the remains of the shipwreck belie the horror of disaster at sea, tucked in a shallow submarine rocky gully leading down onto the sand, half-covered by a canopy of kelp. Of the cargo, roofing slates, glass bottles and various encrusted oddments survive exposed on the surface, now providing a home for a wealth of marine organisms. The anchors that failed the *Elizabeth Anne* can still be seen scattered out on the sand, close to the unforgiving razors of rock that claimed the ship. Of the timber ship itself nothing visible remains, though fragments of the structure may survive beneath the seabed.

**Staigue stone fort**

Staigue fort is one of a number of stone forts, related to ringforts and cahers, which have defensive features shared with Dún Aonghasa on the Aran Islands, and with Doon Fort and the Grianán of Aileach in Donegal. A number of these impressive forts can be found at the western end of the Ring of Kerry, including Loher, Cahergal and Leacanabuile. Staigue fort appears as a circular, drystone enclosure wall or rampart, surrounded by a fosse and external bank, with a causewayed entrance. The walls were

**Above:** Staigue stone fort.

constructed using internal and external faces of roughly coursed drystone masonry enclosing a rubble and fill core. The walls show an external and internal batter, so that they taper from approximately 4m in width at the base to 2m at the top. The stone rampart has a single entrance in the southern quadrant. The trabeate entrance passage has three lintels, with the external lintel relieved by another lintel one course above. The interior of the fort shows two wall-chambers, and the inner face has a series of characteristic X-shaped stairways leading to the top of the walls, a feature also seen in stone forts of Donegal.

Staigue fort was considered unique in the nineteenth century, and the topographer Samuel Lewis devotes a lengthy description to it:

'It stands on a low hill nearly in the centre of an amphitheatre of barren mountains, open from the south to the bay of Kenmare, from which it is about a mile and a half distant. The building, which is nearly of a circular form, is constructed of the ordinary stone of the country, but bears no mark whatever of a tool, having been evidently erected before masonry became a regular art. The only entrance is by a doorway barely five feet high, through a wall upwards of 13 feet

**Above:** Staigue stone fort, by Thomas Westropp (1897).

thick, which opens into an area of about 90 feet in diameter. The circumference is divided into a series of compartments of steps, or seats, ascending to the top of the surrounding wall, in the form of the letter X, and in two of these compartments are entrances to cells constructed in the centre of the wall. The average height of the wall on the outside is 18 feet, battering as it rises by a curve, which produces a very singular effect: the wall also batters on the inside, so as to be reduced from about 13 feet at the bottom to 7 at the top. On the outside the stones are small, and the joints are so filled with splinters of stone as not to be removed without violence. The fort is surrounded by a broad fosse. Various conjectures have been formed as to its origin and use, the most probable of which appears to be that it was erected as a place of refuge for the inhabitants and their cattle from the sudden inroads of the pirates of former times.'

The interior of the caher is slightly raised and was used as a *ceallúnach* or children's burial-ground, a testament to the high rate of infant mortality in the past in Kerry, a harsh reality compounded by the stigma attached to unbaptised children, as until the 1960s it was not permissible to bury unbaptised infants in consecrated ground. These burial-grounds were also used for a wide range of other persons, including suicides, murder victims, people of unknown religion and shipwrecked sailors. Another, older site can be found in the mountainside $c.$ 550m south-south-east of the fort: a primitive copper-mine, appearing as an 8m-wide and 1.6m-high mine face. A 12m-long area of rock art is visible on a large outcrop about 800m south of Staigue fort and about 100m east of a disused bridge.

## Children's burial-grounds

The Ordnance Survey maps show a large number of 'Children's Burial Grounds' on the Iveragh peninsula, and these are a common feature of the Irish countryside.

Originally baptism was intended for adults; widespread acceptance of infant baptism did not begin until the fifth century, when the teachings of Augustine of Hippo emphasised the concept of original sin, and the practice was established in Ireland by the eighth century. Baptism, originally a rite of entry into the Christian church, was now seen liturgically as a washing away of the inherent evil of original sin. Unbaptised children were therefore denied entry into Heaven, and the church introduced the concept of 'Limbo', a place between Heaven and Hell where their souls would go after death. As a consequence, those not absolved of original sin through baptism could not be buried in consecrated ground. The need for separate burial-grounds was well established by the twelfth century. These children tended to be buried alone, at night, by a male member of the family.

Differential treatment of children's burials is not unique to medieval Ireland, but was also a feature of late Neolithic and early Bronze Age Irish society. Children's burial-grounds are marked where known on Ordnance Survey maps, and are often associated with pre-existing archaeological monuments, both early ecclesiastical sites and 'pagan' sites such as ringforts and cahers, often called 'fairy forts'. The association with ringforts is perhaps especially strong as folklore suggests that the fairies were fallen angels, also confined to Limbo. The sites were generally secluded and were usually free from disturbance. Children's burial-grounds were also used for the burial of suicides and murder victims, people of unknown religion and shipwrecked sailors.

**Castlecove Castle**

Castlecove Castle, also known as Bunaneer Castle, stands on a low rocky outcrop overlooking Kenmare Bay and surrounded by scrub and woodland. The castle (really a tower-house) is tricky to access, with a tidal river to the north, the inlet of Castlecove to the east and south, and a marshy area to the west. At high tide the sea comes to within 2m of the east wall of the castle.

The castle is one of the most architecturally decorated tower-houses of the Ring of Kerry. Two storeys of an original three survive, and the battered walls show large quoins (cornerstones) to all angles. All four elevations feature a recessed triangular plane beginning at the batter return, 2.8m above ground level, and increasing in depth as it ascends. The apex of each of these features no longer survives, but they were probably built to facilitate a gun loop. This form of architectural detailing is unusual, but is also known from a surviving example at Ballynamona Castle, Co. Cork. The castle contains ogee- and round-headed limestone windows, with dressed window and door stones. The interior of the castle is accessible though in a ruined condition. The

**Above:** Broken ogee-headed window above the ruined doorway in the west wall of Bunaneer Castle.

**Bottom:** The east wall of Bunaneer Castle, Castlecove, with a recessed triangular plane that may originally have had a gun loop at the apex. The opening at ground level is the discharge from a garderobe (toilet) chute.

original doorway was defended by a murder hole, and the castle shows wall-passages and a spiral staircase in the north-west corner that gives access to the first floor through a pointed-arch stone doorway. The first floor would have been the most luxurious area of the castle, retaining a wide, straight-arched fireplace, and stone corbels show the position of the timber floor. The eastern end of the north wall has a now-blocked lintelled passageway that leads to a basement level.

## Coomnahorna and Garrough stone alignments

Three different but related stone monuments are found within 275m of each other along the upper reaches of the Coomnahorna River, commanding an extensive view along the river valley to Kenmare Bay. Single upright stones are a common feature of the Irish landscape, and the erection of unhewn stones in prominent locations was a widespread custom in eastern and western Europe. These stones are variously noted on Ordnance Survey maps as 'long stone', 'leacht', 'gallan' or 'dallan'. Standing stones range in height from 0.5m to 6m, and some may feature rock art or ogham inscriptions. Examples with the long axis of the stone aligned north-east/south-west suggest an association with stone alignments and circles usually dating from the Bronze Age (2000–800 BC). Standing stones have been erected in all periods for many different purposes, however. Some may have marked prehistoric burials, while others may have functioned as boundary or route markers, ritual or commemorative monuments, or as scratching posts for cattle.

**Above:** Coomnahorna stone pair.

Standing stones can also be found in pairs and alignments, termed stone rows. Stone rows, believed to date from the Bronze Age (2000–800 BC), generally consist of three or more stones set close together and aligned north-east/south-west. Stone rows are concentrated in counties Cork and Kerry and may have had a ritual, ceremonial or commemorative function. Stone pairs, consisting of two stones set close together and also aligned north-east/south-west, are very closely related and

**Above:** Garrough stone row.

probably served a similar purpose.

In the townland of Coomnahorna East, on the lower slopes of Cahernageeha to the west of the Coomnahorna River, stand two monuments, a standing stone and a stone pair. The standing stone is found in the courtyard of a small farm; it stands 2.1m above ground level and is 0.8m wide, inclining to the south, with a number of packing-stones embedded in the ground at the base. In the middle of a field in front of the farm stands a stone pair, aligned north-east/south-west, 4m apart, with the taller stone at the south-west. The south-west stone is 1.7m high, 1m wide and 0.7m deep. Garrough stone row lies approximately 100m and 275m respectively to the north-east. It consists of four standing stones aligned north-east/south-west and extending for 10.5m, with a stone-faced enclosure 3m to its south-east.

**Ballycarnahan Castle**

Ballycarnahan Castle provides a good example of how the smaller tower-houses can almost melt into the landscape, unnoticed. It stands behind the stables of a modern riding school and can be easily overlooked, as the buildings of the village are all of the same local stone. Only three sides of this rectangular tower-house survive overlooking the sea, showing battered walls and rough quoins. The original doorway was located in the east wall, now partly collapsed, though a portion of the door jambs, lintel and relieving arch above have survived. The castle appears quite simple, with splayed loops for windows and a stairwell with spiral steps in the north-east corner. The stairwell area contains a low splayed opening, possibly a gun loop defending the doorway. Thirteen corbels survive in the internal wall surface of the north and south elevations, indicating that the first and second floors of the castle had timber floors.

**Derrynane caher**

Ringforts and cahers are some of the most numerous monuments in Ireland; up to 60,000 examples survive, of which at least 247 are known on the Iveragh peninsula. Ringforts normally consist of a circular or subcircular area between 25m and 40m in diameter, surrounded by one or more earthen and/or stone banks and fosses. Ringforts are the most widespread and characteristic Irish archaeological field monument, and are usually known as *rath*, *raheen*, *lios*, *dun*, *cathair* or *caiseal*. They are generally dated to the early medieval period, but were in use before this and continued to be used until at least the end of the sixteenth century.

A stone ringfort is termed a cashel, or caher in County Kerry. Cashels have the same function and form as earthen ringforts, and any fosse present tends to be cut from the bedrock. Their construction in dry stone without mortar is usually related to the availability and nature of the local building material. Ringforts and cahers were not usually forts in the military sense but functioned as enclosed farmsteads. Stone cahers range in size and architectural detailing. Some may show souterrains—one or more underground chambers linked by creepways and accessed from ground level by a narrow opening. Souterrains are usually associated with ringforts and cashels but are also found in ecclesiastical sites, and sometimes in isolation. They probably functioned as temporary refuges and storage places.

The caher at Derrynane often passes unnoticed by visitors to Derrynane House as the exterior walls, though beside the path, are covered with vegetation in an area of woodland. The caher consists of a circular drystone enclosure approximately 21m across, and the current entrance is through a gap in the drystone walls, which stand over 3m high in places. The caher features a U-shaped souterrain in the western half of the interior that continues into the caher wall. The souterrain has retained some of the massive roof lintels. Some lintels have fallen into the underground U-shaped passage, while others are displaced and partially buried in sod and vegetation. The eastern half of the passage is heavily overgrown by vegetation.

## Derrynane ogham stone

Derrynane ogham stone is visible from the road, located on marshy ground approximately 14m from a small tidal stream and 30m from the sandy shore. Ogham stones are upright standing stones, carved with an inscription to form commemorative monuments, and are usually associated with ecclesiastical sites. The stones range in height from 1m to 2m, with inscriptions in ogham letters along the edges. The inscriptions follow the general formula of 'A, son of B'. Ogham, named after the Celtic god of writing, Ogimus, represents the earliest written Irish language. The nineteen letters of the alphabet are in the form of lines and notches. The stones are usually dated on linguistic grounds from the fifth to the mid-seventh century AD, though ogham continued in use in developing forms through the medieval period. Approximately 360 ogham stones are known, mainly in Cork and Kerry. The majority were not discovered in their original position. Many have been reused as building stones or lintels and can be found in a range of building types, including souterrains, ringforts and churches. The stone at Derrynane, Co. Kerry, and a further group of seven in Smerwick Harbour, Co. Kerry, were exposed on sandy seashores by coastal erosion. The Derrynane stone was found partially buried on Derrynane strand and was erected in its current position by the Office of Public Works during the 1940s. It consists of a single upright unhewn stone, approximately 2.1m high, 0.5m wide and 0.4m deep, with a weathered inscription in ogham on one edge.

**Left:** The ogham stone at Derrynane was originally found partly buried in the sands, and was re-erected here by the OPW in the 1940s.

## Ahamore Abbey, Abbey Island

The Ring of Kerry is famous for its wealth of Early Christian sites and monuments. Ahamore Abbey was reputedly built by the Augustinians, one of the Continental monastic orders who began establishing houses in Ireland from around the 1140s. These new foundations had distinctive layouts, very different to the earlier monasteries, with a formal arrangement of church, chapter house, parlour, refectory and cloister. The ruins of Ahamore Abbey, known locally as 'Derrynane Abbey', stand on a rocky cliff on the north-east edge of Abbey Island on the west side of Derrynane harbour. Access to the island is possible by crossing the sands at low tide. The ruins consist of a rectangular church building with two adjoining rectangular buildings to the south. The original church at this site was probably founded in the sixth century, and later became a dependency of Dairinis, Youghal, in the later medieval period. The main church building is built on the stone bedrock, overlooking the sea to the east, and the walls normally survive almost to full height. The abbey has carved sandstone doorways and windows; a large, central pointed window, with two slightly smaller pointed flankers, illuminates the east gable, with the sea directly underneath.

**Above:** The east window of Ahamore Abbey on Abbey Island, on the west side of Derrynane Bay.

## Derrynane cannons

Derrynane boasts a natural harbour, and was a natural port of call and harbour of refuge for passing ships. In early 1991, five cannons and two anchors were found by a local scuba-diver in a rocky gully adjacent to the mouth of the harbour in less than 6m of water. Another cannon and anchor were found the following year. The cannons are three-pounders and six-pounders, believed to date from $c.$ 1770, and the anchors are probably late eighteenth- or early nineteenth-century. The site is typical of many coastal archaeological sites on the exposed Atlantic coastline of Ireland, where the only surviving traces of a wrecked wooden vessel are a few substantial iron pieces.

**Above:** One of the five cannons, dating from $c.$ 1770, from a shipwreck outside Derrynane harbour.

## Loher stone fort

Loher stone fort stands on the lower slopes of Farraniaragh Mountain, overlooking Ballinskelligs Bay to the west. The fort, really a defended farmstead, consists of a circular drystone enclosure 20m across, with a circular and a rectangular building in the interior. The 4m-thick drystone enclosing wall is battered on the outside, with a terrace and steps on the inside. The fort is entered from the south-east, through a 4m-long passage roofed with five large stone lintels, similar to the entrance to Staigue fort. The caher features two drystone buildings, a rectangular house standing 1.2m high, and an earlier circular building with a souterrain (an underground passage). The

**Above:** Loher stone fort.

souterrain (now closed) is entered from inside the house and may have been used as a refuge during attack, but could also have functioned as a cold store for food.

**Eightercua stone row**

Eightercua stone row stands on the crest of a low ridge overlooking Lough Currane and Ballinskelligs Bay. Stone rows in Kerry and west Cork tend to be formed of between three and six stones, with the tallest stone often found at the western end. The stone row at Eightercua runs approximately north-east/south-west, aligned with the setting sun on the winter solstice, and is 8.6m long. The tallest stone, standing 2.8m high, is at the south-western end of the row, which forms the north-western perimeter of a sub-oval enclosure defined by an earth and stone bank. A low drystone wall abuts the stone row at either end. The function of stone rows remains unknown. They normally point to the north-eastern and south-western sectors of the sky, and could have been focused on turning-points of the solar or lunar cycles. They may have had some form of ritual or ceremonial purpose, but they appear to occur in isolation and are not associated with other monuments. Few of these rows have been excavated, and the little available evidence is not conclusive, but they are usually considered to be Bronze Age in origin.

**Above:** Eightercua stone row.

**Dromkeare stone row**

Much like stone circles, there are two distinct types of stone rows in Ireland: the large numbers of closely spaced low stones found in Ulster, and the large stones used to form rows in Cork and Kerry. About 80 examples are known, of which fifteen are found in the Ring of Kerry. The Kerry stones are usually of megalithic proportions, containing three to six stones, with the tallest stone found at the south-western end.

Dromkeare stone row is found on the edge of a small farm, overlooking Lough Currane to the south, with Eightercua stone row on the far side of the lake. The row

**Above:** Dromkeare stone row, overlooking Lough Currane.

is composed of four stones aligned approximately north-east/south-west and is 7m long. The tallest stone, or orthostat, stands 2.5m high and is positioned at the south-western end of the row. The other stones are of irregular heights, and are secured in place by a number of packing-stones embedded in the ground at the base of each orthostat.

**Ballinskelligs Castle and abbey**

The Skellig monks were forced by deteriorating climatic conditions to abandon year-round life on the Skellig rocks in the middle of the eleventh century, and founded a new church on the mainland in Ballinskelligs Bay. With the reorganisation of the Irish church from the twelfth century, this site became a priory of the Arroasian Canons of the Order of St Augustine in 1210, and is one of the few examples of Continental houses on the peninsula. The priory retained possession of the monastery on the Skellig rocks, and developed buildings on the shores of Ballinskelligs Bay from the thirteenth to the fifteenth century. The monks continued to use the Skelligs until the order was dissolved in 1578. The simple nave-and-chancel church has been broken open by the sea, and the visitor is greeted by the chancel arch with a belfry above. The church has a 'Prior's House' to the north, with the refectory and ruined cloister to the

**Above:** Ballinskelligs Abbey and peat from a submerged landscape emerging from the sands.

**Above:** Ballinskelligs Castle, accessible at low tide, on the west side of Ballinskelligs Bay.

south-west. Many buildings and some of the enclosure and graveyard have been lost over the centuries to constant erosion by the sea, and the destruction of the cruciform church can be clearly seen in a plan of the abbey drawn by P. J. Lynch in 1902.

Very little is known about nearby Ballinskelligs Castle, believed to have been one of the McCarthy castles. It stands in an exposed coastal location on rock outcrop foundations at the end of a south-west-trending storm beach extending to Ballinskelligs Priory, on the west side of Ballinskelligs Bay, and can be easily reached at low tides. The land around the castle has gradually been lost over the years, and the storm beach and cobbles now reach to the foot of the main door. The castle consists of a three-storey rectangular tower-house showing a base batter, and is entered by a ground-floor doorway in the south-east elevation, with access to the upper floors through stairways located in the southern angle of the wall fabric. The pointed-arch dressed sandstone doorway originally featured an iron grille or yett for defence. The entranceway contains a murder hole above, a mural chamber on the right and a mural stairway to the left. The castle is lit by loops with rectangular lintelled embrasures. The south-east and north-west elevations feature a large lintelled window at first-floor level, but these appear to be later insertions into the wall fabric. The walls are built of rubble masonry with roughly dressed quoins or cornerstones, characteristic of medieval ecclesiastical buildings. The walls taper in thickness from over 4m on the ground floor to only 0.7m at second-floor level.

## The Skelligs

The Skelligs are home to perhaps the ultimate expression of Christian ascetic monasticism in Europe. There are two Skellig islands, sharp, towering crags of rock at the edge of the medieval Christian world. The smaller is home to thousands of gannets, with cannons from a forgotten shipwreck in a gully 33m below the waves. The larger island, Skellig Michael, is home to a monastery which legend tells us was founded by St Fionan in the sixth century. The earliest references are to the death of 'Suibni of Scelig' in the eighth century and to a Viking raid in the Annals of Innisfallen for AD 824, when 'Scelec was plundered by the heathens and Etgal was carried off into captivity, and he died of hunger in their hands'.

**Above:** 'The Monastery', by Thomas Westropp (1897).

The wave of Christian monasticism in Europe was led by the ideal of going into exile for the love of God, *peregrinatio pro Dei amore*, and had its conceptual roots in the belief that greater understanding of and union with God could be achieved by withdrawing from civilisation into harsh and isolated regions. This withdrawal from the world could also be achieved by groups of ascetics who would live separately but in close proximity to each other, meeting for religious services. In the Levant and Egypt this led to solitary lives of prayer, in Europe to hermitages perched on almost inaccessible crags in the mountains, and in Ireland to the Skelligs.

The hermitage at Skellig Michael is one of the most isolated places in Europe, a towering craggy rock with stone buildings clinging to narrow ledges 700ft above an unforgiving sea. The rock is spilt into two dramatic peaks, divided by a U-shaped valley known as 'Christ's Saddle'. The north-eastern peak rises to a height of 185m

Skellig Michael—Plan of Monastery.

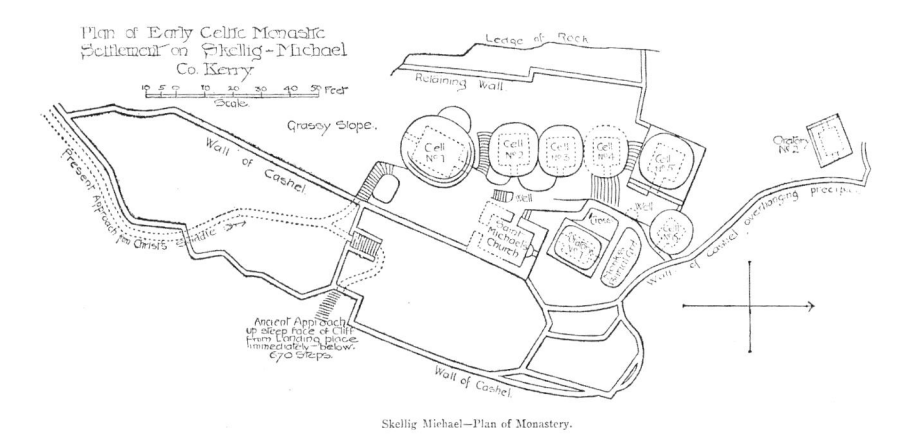

**Above:** Plan of the monastic site on Skellig Michael, by Thomas Westropp (1897).

and holds the main monastery with its stone oratories, beehive huts and 'Monks' Garden' on a terraced shelf. The South Peak, rising to 218m, holds the remains of a hermitage with a stone oratory rediscovered by the nineteenth-century antiquarian Lord Dunraven, who noted: 'near the highest point of the island, which is called the spit, I found the remains of a little building which appears to be quadrangular, probably an oratory'. The island was, at best, challenging to live on, and the climatic downturn of the thirteenth century caused by an expansion of the polar ice cap probably made year-round life on the island impossible. The monks moved to Ballinskelligs Bay, but returned to maintain and use the island until the monastery was dissolved in 1578, and a lease for 'a small islande called SkelligMichell, alias S. Crucis, with a chapel on it' transferred the island to private ownership. The island continued in use as a place of pilgrimage, and Charles Smith in 1756 recounts the dramatic climb to the high North Peak through a narrow rock chimney called the 'Needle Eye' and the spit, 'a long, narrow fragment of the rock, projecting from the summit of this frightful place, ever a raging sea', to reach the monastery.

## VALENTIA ISLAND

Valentia Island is one of the most unusual places in Ireland, perched on the edge of the Atlantic and only joined to the mainland by the bridge at Portmagee in 1970. The island has had close links with Spain by sea, with cattle, skins and tallows being exported and the ships returning with wine and salt. By the sixteenth century the island was part of the lands of the McCarthy Mór, and it changed hands through the generations until leased in 1752, and later bought, by the Fitzgerald family, the knights of Kerry. The other major landowner, Trinity College Dublin, had obtained the townlands of Cool and Tinnies, which formed part of an extensive estate that also incorporated Cahersiveen and Portmagee. The island retains traces of activity from all periods, including megalithic tombs, standing stones, the Early Christian church, a medieval village, the slate quarry and the designed village of Knightstown; children's burial-grounds are found throughout the island. Also of interest is an entirely natural geological monument composed of the fossilised footprints of a tetrapod (four-footed animal) that lived around 385 million years ago and left the water environment to traverse some mud-flats, leaving a trackway of footprint impressions. The site has gained international recognition as it is the oldest *in situ* evidence in the world of the evolutionary transition from aquatic to air-breathing land environments—the first fossil evidence of an amphibian. The site is found on the water's edge, close to the lighthouse and standing stone at Glanleam, on a north-facing coast on the eastern side of Reenadrolaun Point at the northern extremity of Valentia Island.

**Glanleam standing stone**

Glanleam standing stone is located in an exposed coastal environment at Fort Point at the north-east end of Valentia Island and is surrounded by semi-natural grassland. It stands within the defences of Cromwell's Fort, a stone blockhouse of apsidal plan built *c.* 1653 on a promontory to control the approaches to Valentia Harbour and currently the site of the nineteenth-century lighthouse. The standing stone, approximately 3.5m high, 1.4m wide and 0.3m deep, is one of 95 found on the Iveragh peninsula. It is partially supported by a smaller stone standing at an angle.

**Cool East wedge tomb**

Cool East wedge tomb is located on a level terrace on Valentia Island, surrounded by pasture and overlooking the Portmagee Channel to the south, and was first described in 1866 by Alfred Graves. About 505 wedge tombs are known in Ireland, generally containing cremated remains though burials are also known. These megalithic tombs have a gallery constructed with side-stones that decrease in height from the western to the eastern end; the sides either are parallel or have a wedge-shaped appearance. A close-set outer revetment walling emphasises the wedge shape. Wedge tombs are roofed with large stone slabs sitting directly on the upright stone walls of the gallery and are usually aligned north-east/south-west; the entrance, on the east, is often closed by a single stone. Wedge tombs may also feature a portico at the front and a small end-chamber at the rear. The wedge tomb at Cool East consists of a broad chamber roofed by a single capstone slab measuring 3.05m by 2.65m by 0.28m, resting on three orthostats, two on the north side and one on the south side. The side-stones are composed of single stones, but a number of smaller stones fill the spaces between the slabs. The tomb is unusual in its dimensions, and some experts have suggested that the site may previously have been used as an animal shelter or as a temporary dwelling.

**Illaunloughan monastic site**

The eremitical settlement on this small, low-lying island in the Portmagee Channel of Valentia Island is one of nine similar sites situated on offshore islands in the area. The island, which can be reached on foot during certain low tides, contains an oratory, a tent-like gable-shrine surviving within a drystone *leacht*, a circular drystone corbelled hut, a stone-lined well and about 50 upright stone slabs with a possible enclosing wall. The site continued in use into the twentieth century as a children's burial-ground. Recent archaeological excavation revealed an earlier earthen or sod-walled structure beneath the stone oratory, and indicated that the site was a hermitage and did not serve as a community church. Some of the burials on the island dating from the early seventh and mid-eighth centuries were found with whole scallop shells (the emblem of St James), which are linked with pilgrimage routes through Europe to Santiago de Compostela in north-western Spain.

**Cromwell's Fort**

This trapezoidal promontory fort, built *c*. 1653, is located at the western end of the Portmagee Channel and is one of two artillery forts built on Valentia Island during the Cromwellian period. It is cut off from the mainland by a deep, rock-cut ditch and a ravelin (an outwork consisting of two faces forming a salient or projecting angle) with two ditches, and is built on a steep headland that ends in the tidal reef of *sculgaphort* (port cliff). The interior is uneven and the tip of the fort shows the sparse remains of a masonry building. The antiquarian Thomas Westropp wrote in 1912:

> 'The name *Cromwell*, as in eastern Limerick and elsewhere, may have originally referred to a "sloping wood," *Crom-coill*, as the map made by Baptist Boazio, in the reign of Elizabeth I, about 1590, marks "Cromcoel" near the fort'.

**Valentia slate quarries**

The slate quarry opened in 1816 on land leased from Trinity College by the knight of Kerry, and the stone-quarrying was so successful that it led to the design of Knightstown by Alexander Nimmo to export the stone.

The slate was used for a number of purposes. It was used locally for roofing, but the beds were too thick and the slate was consequently not considered ideal for this. The knight of Kerry used his social and political contacts to promote the sale of his slate, resulting in the duke of Wellington's shelving his dairies at Stratfield Saye with Valentia slate, and the Public Record Office in London had 25 miles of Valentia slate shelving made. The slate was very popular for flagging, fish slabs, dairy shelving, tables and billiard tables, and was also used for carved work, including tombstones, fireplaces, tables, seats and wash-stands. A pair of carved Valentia slate benches have been preserved in Tralee Public Library. The stone was transported by small coasters to Dingle, Kenmare, Kilrush, Askeaton etc. The cargo of the shipwreck at Parknasilla largely consists of roofing slate.

The slate was extracted by blasting with gunpowder, and shifted in great blocks; it was lifted by a travelling crane onto wagons, and the rough ends and sides were cut off in the squaring-house just outside the quarry. The blocks were usually 14ft by 6ft for the London market, but could be cut in lengths of up to 20ft or 30ft. The final work was done in the slate yard in Knightstown, where the buildings and the paving were of slate. The quarry employed between 100 and 500 men, depending on the level of production, and was the largest single source of paid employment on Valentia Island in the nineteenth century. The quarry was leased to George Eugene Magnus and his Pimlico Slate Works in 1877. Magnus used steam-powered tools to cut, groove and mould slate into polished items that became very popular with the English nobility. He also developed a technique to apply decorative enamel to slate which won prizes at international exhibitions in the mid-nineteenth century. The most popular item was a patented billiard table, made entirely of slate. A dark slate billiard table can be found in the duke of Wellington's house at Stratfield Saye, and a white enamelled billiard table was ordered by Prince Albert, consort to Queen Victoria, for his new house at Osborne on the Isle of Wight. Billiard tables were sold and transported throughout the British Empire, to Africa, India and Constantinople.

**Cahergal stone fort**

Cahergal stone fort is a circular drystone enclosure built on bedrock exposed on the crest of a ridge. The interior contains a central circular drystone house, two large slabs

**Left:** Valentia slate quarry (Wilkinson 1845).

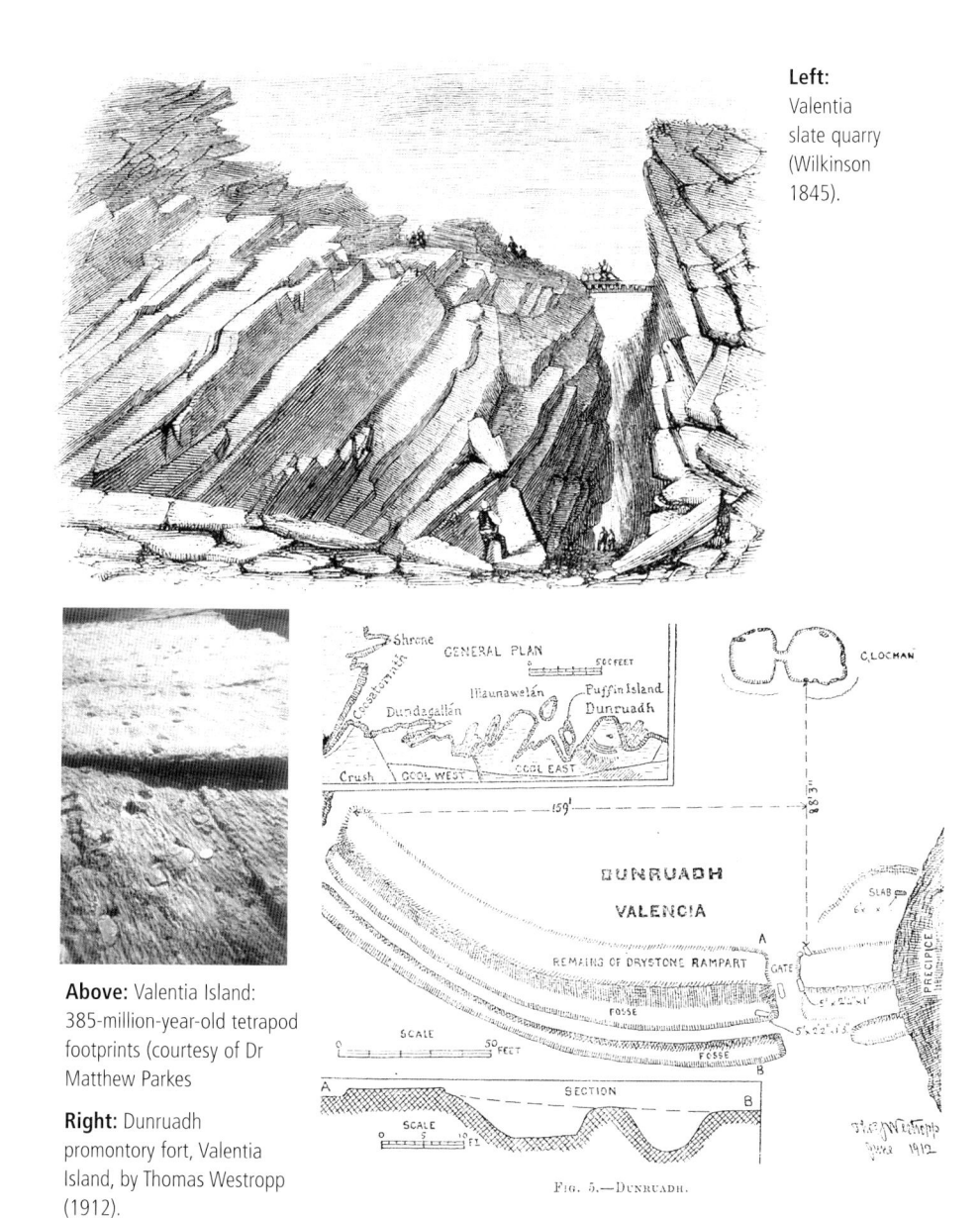

**Above:** Valentia Island: 385-million-year-old tetrapod footprints (courtesy of Dr Matthew Parkes)

**Right:** Dunruadh promontory fort, Valentia Island, by Thomas Westropp (1912).

and a stone cross. The fort is one of three cahers in the area. Cahergal stone fort has recently been restored after archaeological excavations (Manning 1986; 1991). The interior is well-maintained, featuring a lawned area and a gravelled interior to the hut.

The caher is approximately 26.2m wide and can be entered through a reconstructed lintelled passageway in the south-east quadrant. It consists of a circular drystone enclosure wall or rampart, constructed using internal and external faces of

43

roughly coursed drystone masonry enclosing a rubble and fill core. The walls show an external and internal batter, reducing the thickness of the wall from approximately 5.5m at the base to 3.5m at the top.

Internally, the caher wall features two terraces at heights of 1.1m and 2.7m respectively, with a series of nine inset arrangements of opposing steps leading to the top of the walls. The fort contains a ruined central drystone circular building, or *clochán*, which has been reconstructed. The *clochán*, approximately 6.7m in diameter, is accessed through opposing inclined passages in the wall fabric in the south-east and north-west quadrants. It contains a stone cross, resting inverted against the internal face of the house, and two stone slabs lying flat.

**Leacanabuile stone fort**

The caher at Leacanabuile, like the majority of ringforts and cahers, is of early medieval date and functioned as an enclosed farmstead. It was built in the ninth or tenth century on a massive rock outcrop with steep cliffs on three sides, and appears as a circular enclosing wall over 3m thick, containing a round house, a later rectangular house and a souterrain composed of two passages linked by a creep; incised circles and a four-legged animal are carved onto the rock face of the souterrain

**Above:** Leacanabuile stone fort.

**Above:** The rectangular house in Leacanabuile stone fort.

wall. The monument is entered from the east, away from the prevailing winds. The site was excavated between 1939 and 1940 and has been restored. The excavations revealed layers of round and rectangular houses, and finds included iron knives, whetstones, rotary querns for grinding barley or wheat into flour, bone combs, a sickle and a bronze ring-headed pin.

**Ballycarbery hall-house**

Ballycarbery Castle stands on the site of an earlier castle, traditionally attributed to Carbery O'Shea, which reputedly stood here in 1398, but the site is normally associated with the McCarthys. The castle at Ballycarbery is difficult to classify, appearing more similar in design to a thirteenth- or fourteenth- century hall-house than to the smaller tower-houses characteristic of the fifteenth and sixteenth centuries, while retaining architectural features of both these types. The castle overlooks the River Ferta on the east side of Valentia Harbour, and was originally enclosed within a bawn, much of which was dismantled in the early twentieth century. The three-storey building is a rectangular fortified hall with an attached turret at the north-east corner. The castle has battered walls and a round-headed doorway at ground-floor level in the north wall. The interior of the castle is divided into chambers, with pointed

**Above:** The hall, tower and bawn of Ballycarbery Castle on the north shore of the River Ferta, on the east side of Valentia Island.

vaults on wicker centring on the ground floor, and mural stairs giving access to the upper floors. The interior chambers and walls retain beam sockets, wall-cupboards, plaster, round-headed and ogee-headed window openings and other architectural features which allow the layout of the castle to be interpreted. The site has probably been in a ruined condition since it was 'slighted' by Cromwellian forces in 1651–2, when Valentia Harbour was being fortified. The castle was painted by Daniel Grose in the early nineteenth century, and the interior shows gradually tapering walls, vaults, dressed and carved stone, and traces of chambers and stairs. The painting shows the entrance to the castle defended by a portcullis (the groove can still be seen above, served from the second-floor window) and a yett (a steel grille pulled up by chains).

**Kealduff Upper rock art**

There is a wealth of rock art within the townland of Kealduff Upper. The most easily located is a massive, regularly shaped, elongated sandstone boulder, approximately 3m long, 1.5m wide and 0.6m thick, inscribed with cup and circle motifs. The decorated stone lies on a mountain slope approximately 1km above the loughs north of Coomacarrea Mountain, 500m above sea level, surrounded by blanket bog in an exposed upland environment. A further six pieces of rock art can be found scattered in the bog.

**Above:** Rock art at Kealduff Upper, one of the largest concentrations of petroglyphs in Ireland.

## Cloonmore megalith

Cloonmore megalithic tomb is located in a picturesque pasture and consists of a massive roof stone resting on two portal stones. The tomb appears slightly disturbed: the roof stone inclines to the west and the southern portal stone inclines heavily to the south, while the northern portal stone stands in an upright position.

**Left:** The massive sloping roof stone and the northern portal stone of the Cloonmore megalithic tomb.

### Dunloe ogham stones

This site comprises eight ogham stones set in a semicircular arrangement on the side of a local road, erected by the Department of the Environment, Heritage and Local Government. The stones were largely collected from a souterrain in Coolmagort, Co. Kerry, within the demesne of Dunloe Castle, where they had been reused as roof lintels, though one of the stones came from the church of Kilbonane. The souterrain, discovered in 1838, contained burials comprising skulls and other human bones. The arrangement of the ogham lintels was recorded by John Rhys in 1903; the engravings record that parts of the inscriptions could not be seen but only felt, and that one ogham stone was used as an upright prop to support the roof of the passage. Each of these upright unhewn stones bears an ogham inscription. The stones may originally have marked a place of burial, and the inscription on the side of each generally follows the formula 'A son of B'.

### Aghadoe round tower and Romanesque church

Aghadoe lies 3km north-west of Killarney town, overlooking the lakes and the mountains to the south. The remnants of this monastic settlement, reputedly founded by St Finian in the sixth century, can still be traced, containing a round tower, a ruined medieval church and an ogham stone within the graveyard enclosure. The Anglo-Norman castle of Parkonavear is found to the south-west of the site.

Only the base of the round tower survives, a mere stub of 21 courses of masonry, showing a number of different repairs over the years. The tower was photographed in a much more intact condition *c.* 1875. The original part can be seen as an area of large, regular, red-cream blocks of sandstone, laid out as regular ashlar masonry closely fitted together. The original stonework is not exactly level but starts to wobble off-centre around the eleventh course. The masons obviously realised their mistake as they managed to straighten the masonry a few courses higher.

The enclosure also contains a medieval church, dated to 1158 in the Annals of Innisfallen, currently comprising a Romanesque doorway, the west, north and east gables and a portion of the south elevation, which was probably reconstructed. The nineteenth-century term 'Romanesque' was applied to European architecture of the eleventh and twelfth centuries that followed the classical precedents of imperial Roman architecture. European countries such as France, Germany, Italy, Spain, England and Ireland all developed distinct regional styles. In Ireland, the Hiberno-Romanesque style mainly focused on door and window openings and some carved motifs, such as the zigzag or chevron decoration seen on the outer jambs of this

**Above:** The Romanesque doorway at Aghadoe.

doorway. The Romanesque doorway is in three orders and may once have featured a tympanum. The outer ring of arch stones shares the same carved pellet decoration seen in the Romanesque doorway of Kilmalkeadar Church on the nearby Dingle peninsula. The church also has a Romanesque window in the north wall, a number of carved pieces and a deep-green ogham stone laid flat on one of the ruined walls. The smaller of the two carved stones was probably a capital with floral motifs, while the larger bears a Biblical scene showing the Crucifixion with Christ, Mary and an angel.

**Parkonavear Anglo-Norman castle**

The ruins of this thirteenth-century Anglo-Norman castle consist of a cylindrical drum tower or keep, *c.* 6.4m in diameter, within a square earthen rampart defined by an earthen bank and fosse. Anglo-Norman stone fortresses were constructed from about 1180 to 1310, often to replace an earlier timber and earthwork castle erected to defend newly conquered territories. The castles were constructed to a variety of plans as their builders intended them to be unique expressions of lordship. Common features include defensive walls, a keep, drum towers, a defended gatehouse and architectural details such as machicolations, wall-walks, arrow loops and crenellated battlements,

**Above:** The circular keep of the Anglo-Norman castle at Parkonavear, beside the ecclesiastical site of Aghadoe.

features often reproduced on later tower-houses. This castle is one of the few built to a circular rather than a rectangular plan, and is also known as 'the Bishop's Chair' or 'the Bishop's Pulpit', probably owing to its proximity to Aghadoe round tower and church to the north-east. The building is relatively simple, composed of three storeys with walls approximately 2m thick at the base. The keep is entered through a ground-floor entrance; the ground and first floors have lintelled windows and are joined by stairs set into the thickness of the wall. The castle also retains a fireplace from the main hall on the first floor.

**References**

Andrews, J.H. 2003 Sir Richard Bingham and the mapping of western Ireland. *Proceedings of the Royal Irish Academy* **103**C (3), 3–95.

Atkinson, G.M. 1866 Notice of the ogham cave at Dunloe, Co. Kerry. *Journal of the Royal Society of Antiquaries of Ireland* **8**, 523–4.

Atkinson, G.M. 1884 The Cuairt, or stone circle, at Liosvigeen. *Journal of the Royal Society of Antiquaries of Ireland* **16**, 306–7.

Bolton, J. 2007 Submerged ruins. In J. Ashurst (ed.), *Conservation of ruins*, 212–34. Butterworth Conservation Series. Oxford. Elsevier.

Bolton, J. 2008 An assessment of the vulnerability of coastal stone monuments in the Republic of Ireland. Unpublished Ph.D dissertation, Dublin Institute of Technology.

Bourke, E.J. 1994 *Shipwrecks of the Irish coast, 1105–1993*. Dublin. Published privately by the author.

Burl, A. 1995 *A guide to the stone circles of Britain, Ireland and Brittany*. London. Yale University Press.

Carroll, M.J. 2004 *The castles of the kingdom of Kerry*. Bantry. Bantry Studio Publications.

Cotter, C. 2000 The chronology and affinities of the stone forts along the Atlantic coast of Ireland. In J. C. Henderson (ed.), *The prehistory and early history of Atlantic Europe*, 171–9. British Archaeological Reports, International Series 861. Oxford.

Craig, M. 1982 *The architecture of Ireland from the earliest times to 1880*. Dublin. Lambay Books.

Crawford, H. 1922 Ballinskelligs Castle. *Journal of the Royal Society of Antiquaries of Ireland* **53**, 199–201.

Crawford, H. 1926 The early cross-slabs and pillar stones at Church Island, near Waterville, Co. Kerry. *Journal of the Royal Society of Antiquaries of Ireland* **56** 43–7.

Cusack, M.K. 1871 *A history of the kingdom of Kerry*. Dublin. (Reprinted 1995. Eamonn de Burca.)

Day, R. 1884 Stone, copper and bronze antiquities, found near Killarney, silver pyx connected with Tralee, and 14th-century gold finger-ring (not from Kerry). *Journal of the Royal Society of Antiquaries of Ireland* **16,** 281–2.

Dennehy, E.A. 2002 *Dorchadas gan Phian*—the history of *ceallunaigh* in Co. Kerry. *Journal of the Kerry Archaeological and Historical Society* (2nd ser.) **2**, 5–21.

De Paor, L. 1955 A survey of Skellig Michael. *Journal of the Royal Society of Antiquaries of Ireland* **85**, 174–87.

De Valera, R. and Ó Nualláin, S. 1982 *Survey of the megalithic tombs of Ireland. Vol. IV. Counties Cork, Kerry, Limerick, Tipperary*. Dublin. Stationery Office.

Dúchas the Heritage Service 1998 *Record of Monuments and Places. County Kerry*. Dublin. Department of Arts, Heritage, Gaeltacht and the Islands.

Dunraven, Lord 1875–7 *Notes on Irish architecture* (ed. M. Stokes). London. George Bell and Sons.

Finlay, N. 2000 Outside of life: traditions of infant burial in Ireland from *cillín* to cist. *World Archaeology* **13** (3), 407–22.

Fossitt, J. 2000 *Guide to habitats in Ireland*. Kilkenny. The Heritage Council.

Gibbons, M., Barber, D. and Barber, H. 2007 Mesolithic remains discovered on Ross Island, Killarney National Park, Co. Kerry, Republic of Ireland. *Nautical Archaeology* **2007.1**, 4–5.

Gordon, E. 1911 Some Kerry fairies. *Kerry Archaeological Magazine* **6**, 347–56.

Graves, A. 1866 On inscribed monuments in the County of Kerry. *Proceedings of the Royal Irish Academy* **9**, 180.

Horn, W., White-Marshall, J. and Rourke, G.D. 1990 *The forgotten hermitage of Skellig Michael*. Oxford. University of California Press.

Lalor, B. 1999 *The Irish round tower: origins and architecture explored*. Cork. Collins Press.

Larner, J. 2005 *Killarney: history and heritage*. Cork. Collins Press.

Leask, H.G. 1955 *Irish churches and monastic buildings, Vol. I—the first phases and the Romanesque*. Dundalk. Dundalgan Press.

Lynch, P.J. 1894 Discovery of an ogham-stone in County Kerry. *Journal of the Royal Society of Antiquaries of Ireland* **24**, 291–2.

Lynch, P.J. 1900 Church Island, Valentia Harbour, Co. Kerry. *Journal of the Royal Society of Antiquaries of Ireland* **30**, 155–60.

Lynch, P.J. 1902 Some of the antiquities around Balinskelligs Bay, Co. Kerry. *Journal of the Royal Society of Antiquaries of Ireland* **32**, 321–52.

Lynch, P.J. 1903 [1908] Some notes on Church Island, Lough Currane, Iveragh, County Kerry. *Journal of the Royal Society of Antiquaries of Ireland* **38**, 368–81.

Lynch, P.J. 1906 The antiquities of Caherlehillan, Iveragh, County Kerry, *Journal of the Royal Society of Antiquaries of Ireland* **36**, (1906), 276–84.

Manning, C. 1986 'Cahergal', Kimego West. Stone fort. See www.excavations.ie, Database of Irish Excavation Reports, 'Excavations 1986', Kerry 1986:31.

Manning, C. 1991 'Cahergal', Kimego West. Stone fort. See www.excavations.ie, Database of Irish Excavation Reports, 'Excavations 1991', Kerry 1991:070.

Marshall, J.W. and Walsh, C. 1998 Illaunloughan, Co. Kerry: an island hermitage. In M. Monk and J. Sheehan (eds), *Early medieval Munster: archaeology, history and society*, 102–11. Cork University Press.

Mitchell, G.F. 1989 *Man and environment in Valencia Island*. Dublin. Royal Irish Academy.

O'Brien, W. 2000 *Ross Island and the mining heritage of Killarney*. Galway. National University of Ireland, Galway.

O'Cleirigh, N. 1992 *Valentia: a different Irish island*. Dublin. Portobello Press.

O'Flaherty, B. 1985 Loher. Cashel. See www.excavations.ie, Database of Irish Excavation Reports, 'Excavations 1985', Kerry 1985:34.

O'Keeffe, P. and Simington, T. 1991 *Irish stone bridges: history and heritage*. Dublin. Irish Academic Press.

O'Sullivan, A. and Sheehan, J. 1996 *The Iveragh Peninsula: an archaeological survey of south Kerry*. Cork University Press.

Pavía, S. and Bolton, J. 2000 *Stone, brick and mortar: historical use, decay and conservation of building materials in Ireland*. Bray. Wordwell.

Pavía, S. and Bolton, J. 2001 *Stone Monuments Decay Study 2000: assessment of the degree of erosion and degradation of a sample of stone monuments in the Republic of Ireland*. Kilkenny. The Heritage Council.

Pracht, M. 1996 *Geology of Dingle Bay: a geological description to accompany the Bedrock Geology 1:100,000 Scale Map Series, Sheet 20* (with contributions from G. Wright, P. O'Connor, K. Claringbold and W. P. Warren). Dublin. Geological Survey of Ireland.

Pracht, M. and Sleeman, A.G. 2002 *A geological description of West Cork and adjacent parts of Kerry to accompany the Bedrock Geology 1:100,000 Scale Map Series, Sheet 24, West Cork*. Dublin. Geological Survey of Ireland.

Redmond, M. 1999 A survey of the promontory forts of the Kerry peninsulas. *Journal of the Kerry Archaeological and Historical Society* **28**, 5–63.

Rhys, J. 1903 Notes on the ogam-inscribed stones of Donaghmore, Co. Kildare, and Inisvickillane, Co. Kerry, *Journal of the Royal Society of Antiquaries of Ireland* **33**, 75–87.

Shahar, S. 1990 *Childhood in the Middle Ages*. London. Routledge.

Sheehan, J. 1988 Ballinskelligs Castle, Ballinskelligs. Tower house. See www.excavations.ie, Database of Irish Excavation Reports, 'Excavations 1988', Kerry 1988:27.

Smith, C. 1756 [1969 reprint] *The antient and present state of the County of Kerry*. Cork. Mercier Press.

Sweetman, D. 1999 *Medieval castles of Ireland*. Cork. Collins Press.

Swift, C. 2002 Ogham stones in Sligo and their context. In M. Timoney (ed.), *A celebration of Sligo: first essays for Sligo Field Club*, 127–40. Sligo. Sligo Field Club.

Walsh, C. and Marshall, J.W. 2003 *Illaunloughan Island. An early medieval site in*

*County Kerry*. Archaeology Ireland Heritage Guide No. 24.

Westropp, T.J. 1897 Promontory forts and similar structures in the County Kerry. Part II—Kerry coast. *Journal of the Royal Society of Antiquaries of Ireland* **27**, 290–318.

Westropp, T.J. 1910 Promontory forts and similar structures in the County Kerry. Part IV—Corcaguiny (the southern shore). *Journal of the Royal Society of Antiquaries of Ireland* **40**, 265–96.

Westropp, T.J. 1912 Notes on the promontory forts and similar structures in the County Kerry. Part V—Iveragh (Valentia to St Finian's Bay). *Journal of the Royal Society of Antiquaries of Ireland* **42**, 285–324.

Wilkinson, G. 1845 *Practical geology and ancient architecture of Ireland*. Dublin. William Corey Jr and Co.

Woodman, P.C., Anderson, E. and Finlay, N. 1999 *Excavations at Ferriter's Cove, 1983–95: last foragers, first farmers in the Dingle Peninsula*. Bray. Wordwell.